I0766339

The HEALING TREE

A Book of Haikus to Honor One Special Tree

Dave Sandrick, Ed.D.

HEARTS UNLEASHED HOUSE PUBLISHING

Copyright © 2022 Hearts Unleashed House Publishing

Text copyright © 2022 by Dave Sandrick
Cover design by Susan Harring © 2022 by Dave Sandrick
Interior book design by Susan Harring © 2022 by Dave Sandrick

All rights reserved, including the right of reproduction in whole or in part in any form.
First edition, 2022.

For information about special discounts for bulk purchases contact:
hearts@heartsunleashed.com

Manufactured in the United States of America
Library of Congress Cataloging-in-Publication Data Sandrick, Dave.

Summary:

The tree that healed me
It calmed my mind and my soul
And brought happiness

This is a book that celebrates the beauty of nature, and one tree in particular. It caught the eye of one of nature's lost children.

Motivated to get outside after COVID changed how we needed to approach our daily lives, Dave used his walks to connect with nature and do some really impactful soul-searching. Many unresolved thoughts and painful memories were uprooted in his heart during this time and by serendipitously connecting with this one tree, a healing journey was started and continues to this day.

My hope is that THE HEALING TREE will inspire you to find your own connection with the healing powers found in nature and examine the places inside yourself that might need some soothing.

ISBN: 978-1-7376063-4-5 (Hardcover)
ISBN: 978-1-7376063-6-9 (Paperback)
ISBN: 978-1-7376063-5-2 (eBook)

[1. Art 2. Family & Relationships 3. Nature 4. Mind, Body, Spirit 5. Photography 6. Self-Help
7. Lifestyle]

To my parents, who have always provided the
love and support to help me become who I am today.

THANKSGIVING 2021

Why take a picture of the same tree over and over and over again? On one of my first "pandemic walks," it just caught my eye, and then it spoke to my soul, providing a slow, transformative healing. I was taken aback by its simple beauty. It is not necessarily what one might call a perfect specimen of a tree. Well, I am not necessarily what one might call a perfect specimen of a human being.

I've been in need of healing for quite a few years now, but I was as stubborn as that tree is strong. I still am, but I have become less stubborn over time as I let go, little by little, the pain that has not only been caused by others, but also the pain I have inflicted upon myself. There is no need to go into any details of my walk with pain and suffering. We all have been on that walk in one way or another. But not many have had the deep pleasure of experiencing my actual walk along the path at Whihala Beach, off the shores of Lake Michigan, in Whiting, Indiana, where I thankfully encountered this wondrous tree – "My Tree." I know it is not "mine," but it certainly resonated with me, and placed a calmness inside me that I desperately needed.

How did this all happen? COVID came along and forced many to stay in their homes, and forced businesses to shut down. Well, my role as a general manager of a childcare center in Chicago ended in late March of 2020, shortly after my 50th birthday. I had a wonderful time celebrating that milestone with family and friends, surrounded by light, laughter, and love. And then POW! – pandemic. A dark energy tried to break our spirits, which in some ways it did indeed, and many, many lives were tragically impacted in one way or another. That worldwide blast of negative energy took a toll on my psyche. I had just recently moved back to Whiting, my hometown, into a fairly small apartment, and I started to feel very small, as if it was hard to breathe there. So, in April, I started walking to the lake. I needed to be outdoors, to reconnect with nature, and breathe in some fresh air.

Much like Thoreau needed to go "to the woods to live deliberately," (one of my all-time favorite written passages) I needed to go to the lake to live anew. I needed a renewal, a rebirth, a refresher. I needed something. Little did I know that it would be this connection with a tree. And so I photographed it on April 6, 2020. And then again the next day, and the next, each time seeing it anew. I am obviously enamored by the beauty of this tree, but what I came to realize, with time, was that it was everything that surrounded this tree that enhanced its beauty. And then it hit me – my life is enhanced by those who surround me. I live off the energy provided by others, and by nature as well. It is in the lessons I have learned from connecting with the positive energy I find in my interactions with nature that I have learned to generate that positive energy within myself. And then it is the people who surround me who enhance that energy, my own inner beauty, which for many of us is so hard not only to find, but to welcome, embrace, and accept.

I often shared these tree pictures on social media, not only because I wanted to share the beauty I was experiencing with others who were unable to get out of their spaces for whatever reason, but also to encourage others to get outside and walk in some form of nature, to breathe in some fresh air, both physically and spiritually. Many of my friends enjoyed what I shared (at least that's what they were saying—ha ha), and I am sure I got unfollowed by those who grew tired of my pictures. No worries, because I was mainly posting them for my own behalf. To provide a history of my tree walks. And then it hit me, again—these pictures are indeed beautiful, and might make a nice picture book! I could explain to everyone how unique each individual picture was, with the tree slowly changing every single day. But it was the background, that perspective, which was unique every single day, and it deserved some appreciation. Much like us! I believe that if we were all shown a little more appreciation by those around us, we might feel more connected with others, and all of our inner beauties would be enhanced. And maybe, just maybe, the world would be a little better all around. I still love looking at these pictures. I decided to stop at 100 because I thought that was a nice, balanced number. I will continue to take this picture every time I walk by it, with yesterday's picture being the best one yet because my dear child, Ciro, was with me (see below).

I also decided to honor this tree and all that surrounds it by writing a haiku to go with each picture. I love haikus. I love their simplicity, connection with nature, and balance – 5-7-5. I love numbers too, so it just seemed right. Overall, this experience has taught me to be better at getting in touch with my heart and my soul – to love others, and nature, but most importantly, myself, just a little better. It is a slow change, every day, much like this tree, as you will get to see it change through the seasons from Spring of 2020 to now. I needed it all. I think you do too. My hope is that this book will resonate with you somehow, and inspire you to go find your own tree, or lake, or river, or mountain, or whatever will help enhance your life.

So get out there and interact with nature, and hopefully it will encourage you to then connect with your own inner beauty, which will then lead you to share that beauty with others. Take pictures. Share them. Hug that tree if you must, but hugging another human being, especially one who loves you, will be even better. I promise! Thank you so very much for taking the time to read this. I hope you enjoy what follows, and then what is to come.

4-5-2020 (7:33 AM)
Our first connection
Drawn to your beauty and strength
Forever smitten

4-6-2020 (6:20 AM)
Sunrise warms the sky
Highlights the strength of this tree
Strengthening my heart

4-7-2020 (6:13 AM)
Clouds obscure the sun
But soon it will indeed rise
To warm us with joy

4-8-2020 (8:30 AM)
Cloudiness prevails
Blending sky with misty lake
Strengthens your profile

4-9-2020 (6:22 AM)
Beautiful morning
Sunrise breaks the horizon
Hope also rises

4-10-2020 (6:21 AM)
Emerging sunrise
Striking blue darkness lingers
Too deep to fathom

4-11-2020 (6:54 AM)
Iridescent clouds
Blending cool water with sky
Blends mind with the soul

4-12-2020 (6:23 AM)
Promises of Spring
Remain invisible now
Hiding in branches

4-13-2020 (6:14 AM)
Silhouette is strong
Emboldened by pale blue sky
"Stand tall" it beckons

4-14-2020 (6:14 AM)
Anticipation
Builds with the warm rising sun
Happiness abides

4-15-2020 (10:04 AM)
Unseasonable
Snowfall covers warming Earth
Spring grows impatient

4-16-2020 (6:14 AM)
Sun greets the darkness
Casting shadows on the path
Eventually

4-18-2020 (6:13 AM)
This tree does not count
Year, month, day, minute, second
Yet enjoys it all

4-21-2020 (6:03 AM)
Brilliant sun rising
Adding orange to purple
Paints my soul with love

4-23-2020 (6:03 AM)
Peaceful views soothe me
Branches filling in slowly
This pace suits me well

4-26-2020 (5:59 AM)
Colors are lacking
The clouds are dominating
This sadness will fade

4-27-2020 (5:56 AM)
A new day brings hope
This sunrise rewards my heart
Warms by the minute

4-28-2020 (5:51 AM)
Burning glow rises
Strong yet subtle, it awaits
To bathe trees with light

5-1-2020 (5:45 AM)
Darkness feeling cool
This tree stands triumphantly
Conquering the chill

5-2-2020 (5:45 AM)
Tranquil morning wind
Invigorating to breathe
I become the air

5-7-2020 (5:45 AM)
Splendor arises
Thankfulness gently flooding
Eyes, heart, mind, and soul

5-8-2020 (5:41 AM)
Blustery morning
Branches swaying in the breeze
Leaves eager to join

5-12-2020 (11:47 AM)
Sunlight fills my eyes
But I still can see the green
The growth inspires me

5-14-2020 (8:58 AM)
Pale colors surround
Branches filling with green life
Filling me with hope

5-16-2020 (5:28 AM)
Calmness is rising
This sunrise brings peacefulness
This day will be great

5-16-2020 (5:28 AM)
A new perspective
Seeing things in a new light
Helps me feel grateful

5-18-2020 (7:45 AM)
Thickening with green
Emerald buds growing strong
Tree filling with life

5-19-2020 (5:29 AM)
Colorless morning
Some days the sun takes a break
Still so beautiful

5-20-2020 (5:21 AM)
Triumphant return
Morning sun lighting the sky
With warm happiness

5-25-2020 (8:42 PM)
Darkness surrounding
Nighttime brings a different calm
Time to exhale now

5-31-2020 (9:06 AM)
Tree casting shadows
Sees its own strength and beauty
My wish for us all

6-1-2020 (7:50 AM)
Gray clouds surrounding
Tree stands out even more today
Showing off its strength

6-25-2020 (5:13 AM)
Different perspectives
Nice to see this tree has friends
All are connected

6-25-2020 (8:55 PM)
Greenness bursting through
Tree is lush and full of life
Enjoying summer

6-28-2020 (5:46 PM)
Teeming with green life
Tree reaching its potential
Summer suits it well

7-3-2020 (8:26 PM)
Sun taking its time
Setting so much later now
Extends happiness

7-13-2020 (8:23 PM)
Subtly different
But some days things look the same
Consistent beauty

7-17-2020 (6:51 PM)
My shadow stands tall
But not as tall as this tree
I admire its strength

7-19-2020 (8:10 PM)
Soft colors surround
Tree resting in tall grasses
Preparing for sleep

7-21-2020 (5:25 AM)
Summer morning walks
Invigorating the soul
Inspires mindfulness

7-31-2020 (8:09 PM)
Beauty surrounding
Pastel colors lingering
Brings out the tree's strength

8-30-2020 (7:16 PM)
Summer slowly fades
Hints of autumn appearing
New colors coming

10-25-2020 (11:33 AM)
Time passes swiftly
Seasons changed in an instant
Falling leaves come next

10-31-2020 (7:17 AM)
Sun rising later
The tree patiently awaits
New day brings new hope

11-11-2020 (3:47 PM)
Admiration grows
With each photograph I take
This tree heals my soul

11-27-2020 (6:54 AM)
Leaves are all but gone
Silhouette now plain to see
Beauty to the core

12-10-2020 (3:50 PM)
Crisp afternoon air
Lake already looks frozen
Winter will come soon

12-18-2020 (10:52 AM)
Sunlight rules the day
Triumphant over the cold
Brisk air refreshes

2-14-2021 (12:34 PM)
Winter came quickly
But time slipped away moreso
Now watching for spring

2-27-2021 (10:51 AM)
Frigid air remains
The snow wishes to linger
Tree waits patiently

3-7-2021 (9:05 AM)
Azure sky filling
Heart and soul with a deep peace
Its depth unquestioned

3-27-2021 (6:48 AM)
The clouds are awake
Varieties of colors
Enhanced by the sun

4-3-2021 (2:26 PM)
Spring has just begun
Patiently waits for rebirth
Leaves will arrive soon

4-10-2021 (6:12 AM)
Breathtaking sunrise
Unspeakably beautiful
Words will not suffice

4-11-2021 (9:32 AM)
Bluish-gray background
Inviting sadness to come
But the tree says no

4-25-2021 (11:40 AM)
Clouds celebrating
Waves dancing, embracing spring
The tree smiles today

4-30-2021 (7:23 PM)
Absorbing the sun
Sending its warmth as it sets
Smiling is easy

5-11-2021 (5:38 AM)
Streaks of brilliance
Stretch across the horizon
Struggling for words

5-16-2021 (5:28 AM)
The sun is rising
Beyond the comforting clouds
We wait peacefully

5-23-2021 (5:50 PM)
The middle of spring
Has brought this tree back to life
Filling up my soul

5-27-2021 (5:13 AM)
A stunning beauty
I am blessed by this sunrise
Words cannot convey

6-1-2021 (8:14 PM)
Imperfect balance
Yet a perfect connection
Brings me inner peace

6-2-2021 (5:14 AM)
Streaks of radiance
Merge into brilliant sun
My soul is aglow

6-3-2021 (7:21 PM)
Bathing in sunlight
With cool breezes surrounding
A perfect moment

6-10-2021 (7:30 PM)
Setting sun warming
My tree with one final burst
Warms my soul as well

6-13-2021 (5:20 AM)
Early morning sun
The best way to start a day
My heart is renewed

6-18-2021 (3:49 PM)
Daylight makes clearer
The details of every leaf
Simple yet complex

6-18-2021 (8:16 PM)
Pastel sky awaits
The sinking of the sun
So the stars can play

6-20-2021 (8:14 AM)
Moistened air surrounds
Coating my face with cool mists
Sun will wait to shine

6-20-2021 (3:52 PM)
Summer's arrival
Edges closer by the hour
Air filled with sweetness

6-22-2021 (8:10 PM)
Serenity comes
Through breaths of wavy breezes
I am comforted

6-23-2021 (5:16 AM)
Bluish-gray clouds form
Blankets of comfort and peace
Awaiting the sun

6-25-2021 (7:13 PM)
Sunrise came too soon
Yet still you are surrounded
By beauty and light

6-26-2021 (9:32 AM)
Tree is filled with green
We both enjoy the summer
And all that it brings

6-27-2021 (6:20 PM)
Blues are eye-catching
The color reflects my soul
I am in the blues

6-30-2021 (7:20 PM)
Peaceful times are these
My heart is mending slowly
Tree teaching me strength

7-2-2021 (5:35 AM)
Today I feel blessed
Witnessing the sun's splendor
I absorb it all

7-6-2021 (6:03 AM)
Peaceful morning walk
Provides a deep sense of calm
Feel it to the roots

7-8-2021 (9:24 AM)
Colors are faded
Some mornings lack the brightness
The clouds win today

7-13-2021 (7:14 PM)
Sunlight has returned
I understand my soul's need
To bask in its glow

7-20-2021 (7:13 PM)
This scene still inspires
Roots and branches anchor me
Urging me to grow

7-23-2021 (9:34 AM)
Tree providing shade
If only for a moment
I walk to release

8-9-2021 (5:54 AM)
Focusing on its strength
Creates an understanding
That I am strong too

8-25-2021 (6:13 AM)
This beautiful scene
The reason for waking up
Peacefulness rises

9-1-2021 (6:16 AM)
Satisfaction reigns
This brilliant morning's sunrise
Makes everything good

9-4-2021 (9:26 AM)
Imperfect balance
Is what I see every time
But for me it's perfect

9-6-2021 (6:48 AM)
Magnificent dawn
Tree is basking in sunlight
My heart gets a boost

9-6-2021 (7:01 PM)
Such beauty, this scene
Felt compelled to revisit
Duly rewarded

9-14-2021 (7:18 PM)
Focus on the trunk
It is what gives the tree strength
Allowing beauty

9-18-2021 (10:42 AM)
The roots of this tree
Unseen but so meaningful
Anchoring beauty

9-22-2021 (7:23 PM)
Wind makes an attempt
To conquer this tree's resolve
Instead it dances

9-29-2021 (6:22 PM)
Sunset brings new light
Gives a sharpness to this tree
Highlighting its depth

9-30-2021 (10:20 AM)
This tree touched my heart
When I needed some beauty
And a connection

10-2-2021 (9:37 AM)
Coming to the end
These walks have been a blessing
Heart slowly healing

10-9-2021 (10:28 AM)
Glowing with sunlight
Reflecting warmth, hope, and joy
I walk on in peace

10-10-2021 (6:59 PM)
Darkness surrounding
Tree looks stronger in the shadows
Ready for the night

10-12-2021 (8:47 AM)
Autumn peacefulness
Tree waits for its leaves to fall
For now, they hold on

10-19-2021 (7:10 AM)
Colors blend nicely
Sunrise always inspiring
Be better today

10-22-2021 (5:56 PM)
Loneliness in blue
Sometimes the clouds remind me
At least nature helps

10-26-2021 (5:38 PM)
Strong clouds gathering
Amplifying the beauty
Of tonight's sunset

11-24-2021 (10:58 AM)
Thankfulness abides
In my heart and in this place
Two favorites combined

6-22-22 (8:33 PM)
Spirit's warm embrace
Your presence surrounding us
Forever grateful

My dad, James Francis Sandrick, passed away peacefully on this night while Ciro and I rode our bikes to catch the sunset. I took this picture knowing he was in it somehow. When I left the hospice house, I said my goodbyes because I had a feeling the end was near. I told him he did a good job and that I loved him very much. He will always have an impact on me, and I know for a fact that he has had an impact on the community he loved so very much, my hometown of Whiting, Indiana.

Since his passing, many people have reached out to tell me how much of an impact he had on them, some people I didn't even really know. That's all he ever really wanted to do—help people, and to help Whiting be the best place to live and enjoy. He helped teach us to appreciate the great outdoors, and would always tell us, "It's a beautiful day today."

Thanks for helping me understand that, Dad.

This week is my Spring Break. I had taken a very long break from catching a sunrise on a morning walk until a few days ago—March 21, 2022 to be exact. It was so nice to be back out there. And then yesterday, March 22, 2022, I saw a memory on Facebook from two years ago where I went on my first walk to the lake. I didn't start photographing the tree until April of 2020, but the desire to get walking started, and I went with it. As I mentioned in the introduction, these walks, and connecting with that one beautiful tree began a process of a slow, transformative healing. It was brought to my attention during a very wonderful and meaningful chat that I had avoided getting to the root of my own pain and grief. So, this journey of mine was not really completed. I wish to do that now.

I wrote in the introduction that there was "no need to go into any details of my walk with pain and suffering." That right there has historically been a big part of my problem – avoid the pain and the suffering at all costs. Create peace and harmony wherever possible, and if pain and suffering were to find me, quickly replace it with peace and harmony. Well, that doesn't work so well, which I have been unpacking since July of 2016, when pain and suffering came calling.

I do realize that my own tragedy pales in comparison to others, but the experience I had was tragic nonetheless, and I would not wish it upon anyone. I have shared the details many times since July of 2016, and every time I did, it felt very surreal, like it surely did not happen to me. I am a good human being—how could evil have chosen me and my family? Why us? At a time of year that I find great joy, I discovered great pain. I found out in the most gut-wrenching fashion that my marriage was broken and had begun a slow and painful death. This is where I choose to spare the details, just know that an evil force became known to me, and it knocked me out cold. A person who was a "friend" turned out to be a horrible person, had infiltrated my family, and was slowly destroying it all for several years. All the while, I had no clue.

Perhaps that falls back on me for not catching any signs. All I knew was that once everything came to light, I went into denial and avoidance mode and buried the pain as deep as I possibly could. To top it off, I also tried to drown the visions and memories and pain with alcohol, which of course was a very bad decision on my part. Roots continued to dig deeper and deeper. Eventually, what I thought I had successfully buried and conquered would come back to find me, and that happened in July of 2018. For two years I thought I was handling everything so strongly. Sure I had thoughts of hurting the person who had made a selfish, soulless decision to wreck my marriage. Maybe I should have, but what good would that have truly done. I discovered I was not strong enough to forgive and forget and move on with life as if nothing tragic and horrible had happened. But in July of 2018, I broke. The weight I was carrying and the lie I was living wrecked my soul, and I made a decision that would ultimately lead to the end of my marriage.

Unfortunately, this turn of events would make it seem like I had caused the ruin of my marriage and life as we knew it as a family. I didn't plan on it happening this way. Who plans a tragedy? Nobody. You deal with it. Or in my case, you can try to deny it all, or blame others, but ultimately it will all come to light. Well, the facts of my own personal tragedy have not all come to light, and perhaps that should create anger and resentment inside of me. I was angry about that for a while after my divorce was final. I like to think that my walks along the lake and my connection to this tree has led to my successful "tree-covery." I truly believe that has been happening for me since April of 2020. I am still scarred, like when foolish people carve things into trees. I have a mark on my heart that will never go away, but like that marked tree, I will continue to grow, thrive, triumph, and rise above the ashes from a fire I did not start.

Since I started walking and taking pictures of this awe-inspiring tree, I have worked on healing the deep wounds inside of me. It is a work in progress, and when I go on my walks, I give thanks that I am still alive and able to share with others that it is possible to begin again, to live, thrive and survive. And not just survive, but to embrace every experience and learn from each one. To find the positive lesson that our experiences teach us, even if those experiences are painful and heart-breaking. We can heal. Grief will not magically disappear, and it will not be ignored. It can be shared with others, and then you find out that there is magic, and that magic is the love and support of others. I am grateful to the many, many wonderful people who have come into my life, whether it has been for a reason, a season, or a lifetime. I am grateful for the life lessons they have helped me learn, whether I wanted the lesson or not. I hope to now be able to connect and share with others, thanks to this writing and this tree, that love will be one of the most important things you can have and give, as we all continue on our journeys together.

ACKNOWLEDGMENTS

I've already mentioned my mom and dad—none of this would have been possible without them.

To Kate and Ciro—I believed a very long time ago that I was meant to be a dad, and you have been the best thing that could have ever happened to me.

To Abigail—another wonderful human who believed in my ramblings about this project and helped bring it to life. I look forward to the adventures that will follow.

And there are so many other wonderful humans in my life that enhance my life on a daily basis—family, friends, wandering souls. My plan is to contact you all individually and thank you personally. Connecting with others is the fuel that keeps me going in a positive direction.

Growing up surrounded by an aesthetic contradiction; a juxtaposition of nature and industry, Dave learned early on to seek out beauty amongst sometimes challenging views. He continues to walk with and connect to nature for healing and inspiration, and tries to walk by the Lake (Michigan) as often as possible. In his early twenties, he signed up for a social psychology class at Indiana University which sparked a fascination in him for the reasons why people become who they become. This feeling caused him to want to find out how to help people become better people. What better way to help than by becoming a teacher, and a teacher who also loves to write. Maybe, just maybe, this writing will not only help himself make better sense of this crazy world, but help others as well.

Dave went to school for a very long time, and hopes to make a career out of university teaching someday. He has a Bachelor's degree in Elementary Education, a Master's degree in History and Philosophy of Education, and a Doctorate of Education (Ed.D.) in Curriculum and Instruction/Early Childhood Education. He began his career teaching fifth grade at Nathan Hale Elementary School in Whiting, Indiana (his hometown), and after several different career changes in the education field (infant teacher, child care director, executive director, general manager) in Bloomington, Evansville, Indianapolis, Chicago, and now East Chicago, he has come full circle and returned to elementary education back in October of 2021. Thanks to the pandemic of 2020, he rediscovered his passion for photography and writing, and hopes to start blogging about it all very soon. Currently, he is thoroughly enjoying his first summer off in thirteen years.

Dave loves being active, especially walking along Lake Michigan or biking with friends to local watering holes. He loves connecting with people, especially if it is a serendipitous encounter that leads to conversations about intuition and other spiritual ramblings. He especially loves connecting with kids, which has led to twenty-seven years of various teaching opportunities. He returned to Whiting in 2020 and feels a deep contentment that is often hard to find in life, and now feels a sense of peace in his soul. Finally!

www.ingramcontent.com/pod-product-compliance
Lightning Source LLC
Chambersburg PA
CBHW051106300726

48981CB00001B/10